ARE WE THERE YET?

HODDER
Wayland

an imprint of Hodder Children's Books

New Experiences

Are We There Yet? My First Holiday
Can I Feed It? My First Pet
I Want That Room! Moving House
I'm Still Important! A New Baby
Open Wide! My First Trip to the Dentist
Say Aah! My First Visit to the Doctor
Where's My Peg? My First Day at School
Where's My Present? My First Party

Published in Great Britain in 2000 by Hodder Wayland,
an imprint of Hodder Children's Books
© Copyright 2000 Hodder Wayland

Editor: Jason Hook
Designer: Tessa Barwick

A Catalogue record for this book is available from the British Library.

ISBN 0 7502 2669 2

Printed and bound in Italy by G. Canale & C.Sp.A., Turin

Hodder Children's Books
A division of Hodder Headline Limited
338 Euston Road, London NW1 3BH

ARE WE THERE YET?

My First Holiday

Written by Jen Green

Illustrated by Mike Gordon

HODDER
Wayland

an imprint of Hodder Children's Books

Today mum, dad and I woke up early. We were off to the seaside for my first holiday!

We packed our car with bulging suitcases. Then we squeezed in too.

We waved goodbye to our neighbour Joan, who was looking after our cat Ginger.

6

Then we were off. I had never been to the seaside. What would it be like?

The car journey was long and boring.
I ate some sweets ...

then I felt sick.

'Are we there yet?' I asked.

But mum said we wouldn't get there for ages.

9

At last we arrived at a campsite near the sea. The air smelt salty. We put up our tent as it got dark.

Then dad cooked
sausages for tea.

Mum tucked me up in my sleeping bag,
but our tent was full of spiders!

I missed my own room, and I missed Ginger. It was hard to get to sleep.

Next day we went down to
the sea at last. It was much
bigger than I expected.

It sparkled and stretched on for ever.
You couldn't see the other side.

Mum and I went paddling. The water was very cold at first.

Later I put
on my water-wings,
and Dad helped me to swim.

Most days were hot and sunny.
I made sand-castles with
a girl called Sam.

We buried dad in the sand ...

and surprised mum
with a crab.

One day we went to a theme park with Sam and her family.

The park was
brilliant! Sam and
I went on lots of rides.

Suddenly I couldn't see mum, dad,
or anyone I knew.

I felt scared, but I didn't panic. Then a woman stopped and asked me if I was lost.

The woman took me to
an information point.

The man there spoke into a microphone, telling mum and dad to fetch me. His voice boomed everywhere.

Mum and dad rushed up and hugged me. Then we all went for a pizza.

All too soon our holiday was over, and I had to say goodbye to Sam.

The journey home took even longer. At last our house appeared, and Ginger was waiting.

Our holiday had been great, but it was good to be back home.

Notes for parents and teachers

This book introduces children to the experience of going on holiday. Parents or teachers who read the book with children may find it useful to stop and discuss issues as they come up.

Holidays are fun, but they introduce new settings and unfamiliar situations. New challenges may include practical matters such as finding the way round new places, eating different kinds of food, learning new skills and taking in a lot of information.

Emotional challenges may include meeting new people, coping with change, and learning to compromise. Some children find it hard not to be the centre of attention or get their own way all the time, but learning to consider others is part of growing up.

Long journeys can be a trial for both adults and children. Prepare games and activities that can be played in the car to avoid boredom, or provide bedding so children can go to sleep. Break up long journeys with stops.

Children who have been on holiday might like to talk or write about their own experiences, using the book as a framework.

How did the children's holidays differ from the one described in the book? Children could write accounts or make up fictional stories about their best or worst holiday. The stories could be put together to make a class book.

The experience of going on holiday may introduce children to unfamiliar words or phrases, including: campsite, pitching a tent, camping stove, sleeping bag, water-wings, theme park, microphone. Make a list of all the new words and discuss what they mean.

Use this book for teaching literacy

This book can help you in the literacy hour in the following ways:

- ✓ Children can write simple stories linked to personal experience using the language of the text in this book as a model for their own writing. (Year 1, Term 3: Non-fiction writing composition.)

- ✓ Children can look through the book and try to locate verbs with past and present tense endings. (Year 1, Term 3: Word recognition, graphic knowledge and spelling.)

- ✓ Use of speech bubbles shows a different way of presenting text. (Year 2, Term 2: Sentence construction and punctuation.)

Books to read

Wish You Were Here by Martina Selway (Red Fox, 1994)
Rosie goes on the school camp, and writes home about
her experiences. At first, she hates it. It's always raining
and everything is muddy. Later the sun comes out, and
Rosie begins to have a good time.

Lucy and Tom at the Seaside by Shirley Hughes
(Puffin Books, 1976) Lucy, Tom and
their parents go on a train journey to
the seaside. At the beach, they have
a great time, and even fit in a
donkey ride.

A Really Great Time by Helen
Oxenbury (Walker Books, 1984)
Three stories about holidays and
visits that don't quite turn
out as planned, including a
story about a long journey
that becomes
a nightmare!